BUILDING BLOCKS OF ELECTRONIC.

A Practical Guide for Future Tech Leaders

Golf Ofuka

gcodecloud GmbH

Copyright © 21.12.2024 gcodecloud GmbH

All rights reserved

The characters and events portrayed in this book are fictitious. Any similarity to real persons, living or dead, is coincidental and not intended by the author.

No part of this book may be reproduced, or stored in a retrieval system, or transmitted in any form or by any means, electronic, mechanical, photocopying, recording, or otherwise, without express written permission of the publisher.

ISBN-13: 9798304544238
ISBN-10: 9798304544238

Cover design by: gcodecloud GmbH
Printed in the United States of America

Dedication

To The Lord Jesus and my family—your unwavering love, support, and belief in me have been the foundation of my resilience and success.

To my team at gcodecloud GmbH and Mega Phonebook Nig—this is for your dedication, passion, and commitment to turning vision into reality.

To every tech leader, entrepreneur, and dreamer navigating the challenges of innovation—may this book inspire you to lead with courage, resilience, and purpose.

This is for those who dare to build, to lead, and to transform the future.

CONTENTS

Title Page
Copyright
Dedication
Introduction
Chapter 1   1
Chapter 2   7
Chapter 3   13
Chapter 4   22
Chapter 5   30
Chapter 6   36
Chapter 7   42
Chapter 8   48
Chapter 9   55
Chapter 10   61
Chapter 11   67
Chapter 12   74
Acknowledgement   81
About The Author   83

INTRODUCTION

Electronics are at the heart of our rapidly advancing technological world. From the devices we use daily to the innovations shaping industries, electronics form the invisible backbone driving progress. For tech leaders and business innovators, understanding the fundamentals of electronics is more than just a technical skill —it's a strategic necessity.

The Building Blocks of Electronics: A Practical Guide for Future Tech Leaders is designed to provide you with the knowledge and tools to navigate this essential field, whether you're a leader in a tech start-up, managing innovation in a corporate environment, or preparing to guide a team into uncharted technological territories.

Why Electronics Matter to Leadership

Electronics are no longer the sole domain of engineers and technicians. Today, leaders across industries need to understand how electronic systems work to make informed decisions, inspire innovation, and stay ahead of the curve. The ability to discuss circuit design, hardware components, or energy efficiency with your team or stakeholders not only strengthens your leadership but also ensures your business decisions are rooted in a solid understanding of the technology that drives your products or services.

As a tech leader, your role isn't necessarily to design circuits or assemble components, but to lead teams that do. This requires a foundational knowledge of electronics to ask the right questions, foster collaboration, and translate technical challenges into strategic opportunities.

Bridging the Gap Between Knowledge and Strategy

This book aims to simplify the complexities of electronics while connecting them to leadership and business strategy. It's not a textbook filled with equations and jargon, but a practical guide that explains how electronics work and how this knowledge can empower you as a leader. You'll learn how components like resistors, capacitors, and microcontrollers combine to create systems that drive innovation. More importantly, you'll see how these systems can be leveraged strategically to shape the future of your organization.

What You'll Gain

By the end of this book, you'll have a clear understanding of:

- The foundational principles of electronics, broken down into accessible concepts.
- The practical applications of electronics in solving business and societal challenges.
- How to approach electronic systems strategically to drive innovation and growth.
- Emerging trends in electronics, such as IoT, smart devices, and renewable energy, and how they can transform industries.
- Leadership insights to bridge technical knowledge with visionary decision-making.

A Leader's Journey

As someone deeply involved in technology and business, I

understand the challenges leaders face when bridging technical knowledge with strategy. This book is the product of my own journey in navigating the world of electronics and finding ways to align it with business innovation. My goal is to help you build the confidence to engage with your technical teams, understand emerging opportunities, and lead with both vision and competence.

Whether you are just starting to explore electronics or seeking to deepen your understanding to support your leadership, this book is here to guide you. It's time to unlock the potential of electronics and use it as a stepping stone to transform ideas into reality.

Let's embark on this journey together, building the blocks of knowledge and leadership that will define the future of technology.

CHAPTER 1

INTRODUCTION TO ELECTRONICS

What is Electronics?

Electronics is a branch of physics and electrical engineering that deals with the study and application of devices and systems that manipulate electrical energy. At its core, electronics involves the flow of electrons through various materials to achieve specific functions and results. This field encompasses a wide array of components, including resistors, capacitors, diodes, transistors, and integrated circuits, each playing a crucial role in the operation of electronic devices. Understanding these components is fundamental for computer students and engineers, as they form the building blocks of all electronic systems, from simple circuits to complex computing devices.

The history of electronics dates back to the late 19th and early 20th centuries, marked by significant inventions such as the vacuum tube and the transistor. The vacuum tube, initially used in radio technology, paved the way for the development of early computers. However, it was the invention of the transistor in 1947 that revolutionized electronics, allowing for smaller, more efficient, and reliable devices. Transistors replaced vacuum tubes in many applications and are now foundational elements in nearly all modern electronic devices, from smartphones to supercomputers. This historical context is essential for tech founders and engineering students as it highlights the evolution of technology and sets the stage for future innovations.

Electronics can be categorized into two main branches: analog and digital electronics. Analog electronics deals with continuous signals and variable voltages, commonly found in devices such as radios and amplifiers. In contrast, digital electronics works with discrete signals, typically represented in binary code, which is essential for computers and microcontrollers. The distinction between these two branches is critical, as each has its unique principles, applications, and design methodologies.

Understanding the differences allows students and aspiring tech leaders to choose their areas of focus and specialization in their educational and professional journeys.

In practical applications, electronics plays a pivotal role in a wide range of industries, including telecommunications, consumer electronics, automotive, healthcare, and renewable energy. The integration of electronic systems has transformed the way we communicate, work, and live. For instance, advancements in electronics have led to the development of smart devices that enhance connectivity and efficiency in everyday tasks. Moreover, the rise of the Internet of Things (IoT) illustrates how electronic components can be embedded in various objects to collect and share data, leading to smarter and more automated environments. This interconnectedness highlights the significance of electronics in shaping future technologies and innovations.

As technology continues to advance, the importance of electronics in various fields will only grow. For computer students, engineers, and tech founders, gaining a solid understanding of electronic principles and components is essential for driving innovation and developing solutions that meet the demands of an increasingly digital world. Embracing the fundamentals of electronics not only equips individuals with the necessary skills to build and design sophisticated systems but also fosters a mindset of innovation that is crucial for leading in the tech industry.

Importance of Electronics in Technology

The importance of electronics in technology cannot be overstated, as it serves as the foundation for nearly all modern devices and systems. Electronics encompasses a range of components, such as resistors, capacitors, diodes, and transistors, which are essential for controlling the flow of electricity. These components form the basis of circuits that enable devices to function effectively. From smartphones and computers to automotive systems and household appliances, the role of electronics is pivotal in facilitating the operation and connectivity of these technologies.

One of the primary reasons electronics is crucial in technology is its ability to enhance functionality and performance. Through the miniaturization of electronic components and the integration of circuits, devices have become increasingly powerful and efficient. Innovations in semiconductor technology, for instance, have led to the development of microprocessors that can perform billions of calculations per second. This has allowed for advancements in artificial intelligence, machine learning, and complex data processing, which are foundational to the next generation of technological applications.

Moreover, the versatility of electronic components allows for the creation of a wide variety of devices tailored for specific functions. In fields such as telecommunications, electronics enable the transmission and reception of data over vast distances. This capability is essential for the operation of the internet, mobile networks, and satellite communications. Similarly, in the realm of consumer electronics, the integration of sensors and microcontrollers has given rise to smart devices that can interact with users and other devices, providing a seamless experience that enhances daily life.

The impact of electronics extends beyond consumer products into critical areas such as healthcare and environmental monitoring. Electronic devices such as medical imaging equipment, wearable health monitors, and diagnostic tools have revolutionized patient care and treatment. These technologies rely on sophisticated electronics to provide accurate readings and enable real-time data analysis, which can lead to better health outcomes. In environmental monitoring, electronics play a key role in collecting and processing data related to pollution levels, climate change, and resource management, contributing to informed decision-making and sustainable practices.

Finally, as future tech leaders, understanding the importance of electronics in technology equips students and aspiring engineers with the knowledge needed to innovate and solve real-world problems. The intersection of electronics with other disciplines, such as computer science, mechanical engineering, and materials science, opens up numerous opportunities for interdisciplinary collaboration. By mastering the principles of electronics, students can contribute to the development of cutting-edge technologies that push the boundaries of what is possible, ultimately shaping the future landscape of technology.

Overview of Basic Concepts

Electronics is a vast field that encompasses various principles and concepts essential for understanding how devices function. At its core, electronics deals with the behavior of electrons in different materials and how these behaviors can be harnessed to create functional systems. Basic concepts such as voltage, current, resistance, and power form the foundation of electronic principles. Comprehending these terms is crucial for any aspiring tech leader, as they provide the building blocks for more complex systems and circuits.

Voltage, often referred to as electrical potential, is a measure of the potential energy per unit charge available to drive electrons through a circuit. It is analogous to the pressure in a water system that pushes water through pipes. Current, on the other hand, is the flow of electric charge, typically measured in amperes. Understanding the relationship between voltage and current is critical, as it dictates how much power is available for devices and how components interact within a circuit. The application of Ohm's Law, which connects voltage, current, and resistance, serves as a fundamental tool for analyzing and designing electronic circuits.

Resistance is another essential concept, representing the opposition to the flow of current within a material. Every material has a specific resistivity, determining how easily current can pass through it. Components such as resistors are designed specifically to introduce resistance into circuits, enabling the control of current flow and voltage distribution. Recognizing how resistance affects circuit behavior is vital for troubleshooting and optimizing electronic systems. Additionally, it is important to understand series and parallel circuits, as these configurations significantly impact overall resistance and current distribution.

Power, defined as the rate at which energy is consumed or produced, is a critical concept in electronics. It is calculated as the product of voltage and current, signifying how much energy is used by a device over time. The efficient management of power is essential in electronic design, especially in battery-operated devices where energy conservation is paramount. Understanding power ratings and consumption allows tech leaders to make informed decisions regarding component selection and system design, ultimately leading to more sustainable and efficient technologies.

Lastly, the interplay between these basic concepts lays the groundwork for more advanced topics such as circuit design, signal processing, and microcontroller programming. Mastery of the foundational principles enables students and future tech leaders to venture into specialized areas with confidence. As technology continues to evolve, a solid grasp of these basic concepts will empower individuals to innovate and lead in the ever-growing field of electronics. Emphasizing the importance of these fundamentals will not only enhance technical skills but also foster a deeper understanding of how electronic systems shape our world.

CHAPTER 2

FUNDAMENTAL CONCEPTS OF ELECTRICITY

Voltage, Current, and Resistance

Voltage, current, and resistance are fundamental concepts in electronics that form the backbone of how electrical circuits operate. Voltage, measured in volts, is the potential difference that drives electric charge through a circuit. It can be thought of as the force that pushes electrons through a conductor. Understanding voltage is crucial for anyone involved in electronics, as it determines how much energy is available to perform work within a circuit. In practical applications, voltage can vary widely depending on the circuit design and the components used, from low-voltage batteries in portable devices to high-voltage systems in industrial machinery.

Current, measured in amperes, refers to the flow of electric charge in a circuit. It represents the actual movement of electrons and is influenced by both the voltage applied and the resistance present in the circuit. Current can be direct (DC) or alternating (AC), each with its own applications and characteristics. For computer students and engineers, comprehending current is essential for designing and troubleshooting circuits, as it can affect everything from the performance of microcontrollers to the efficiency of power supplies. Additionally, understanding how current behaves under different conditions helps in the selection of appropriate components that can handle the desired load.

Resistance, measured in ohms, is the opposition that a material presents to the flow of electric current. It is an intrinsic property of materials and is influenced by factors such as temperature, material composition, and physical dimensions. Ohm's Law, which states that voltage equals current multiplied by resistance ($V = I * R$), is a fundamental principle that illustrates the relationship between these three quantities. This law is not only vital for circuit analysis but also critical for predicting how changes in resistance will affect current and voltage in a circuit.

For tech founders and engineers, mastering this relationship is key to innovating and optimizing electronic designs.

In practical applications, understanding the interplay between voltage, current, and resistance enables the design of more efficient circuits. For instance, in power management systems, engineers must ensure that the voltage levels are appropriate for the components used, while also managing the current to prevent overheating and damage. Similarly, in digital circuits, the precise control of voltage and current is necessary to ensure reliable operation of logic gates and microprocessors. As technology advances, the demand for efficient circuit design will only grow, making it essential for future tech leaders to grasp these basic electronic principles.

Finally, the implications of voltage, current, and resistance extend beyond individual components to entire systems. In complex electronic devices, such as smartphones and computers, understanding these concepts allows for the integration of various technologies into cohesive systems. By utilizing voltage regulation techniques, current limiting, and resistance matching, engineers can create devices that are not only functional but also energy-efficient. As students and future leaders in technology, a solid grasp of these foundational concepts will empower you to innovate and lead in the rapidly evolving field of electronics.

Ohm's Law

Ohm's Law is a fundamental principle in electronics that describes the relationship between voltage, current, and resistance in an electrical circuit. Formulated by the German physicist Georg Simon Ohm in the 1820s, this law is essential for understanding how electrical components interact. The law is mathematically represented by the equation $V = I \times R$, where V represents voltage measured in volts, I represents current measured in amperes, and R represents resistance measured in ohms. This equation serves as the backbone for analyzing and designing circuits, making it a critical topic for students and professionals in electronics.

In practical terms, Ohm's Law can be applied to various electronic components, including resistors, capacitors, and inductors. When designing a circuit, understanding how these components behave under different voltages and currents is crucial. For instance, if you know the resistance of a resistor and the voltage applied across it, you can easily calculate the current flowing through it using Ohm's Law. This calculation is vital in ensuring that components operate within their specified limits, preventing damage and ensuring reliable performance.

Ohm's Law also plays a significant role in troubleshooting electronic circuits. When a circuit malfunctions, engineers often use this law to diagnose issues related to improper voltage or current levels. By measuring the voltage across a component and assessing the current flowing through it, technicians can identify whether components are functioning as intended or if they are failing. This practical application of Ohm's Law streamlines the repair process and enhances the efficiency of electronic systems.

Furthermore, Ohm's Law extends beyond simple circuits, influencing more complex systems such as power distribution networks and integrated circuits. In these applications, engineers must consider not only the basic relationships outlined by Ohm's Law but also the effects of temperature, frequency, and non-linear components. Understanding these factors is crucial for developing advanced technologies that rely on precise electronic control and signal processing.

In summary, Ohm's Law is a foundational concept that every computer student, engineer, and tech founder should master. Its applications range from basic circuit design to troubleshooting and advanced electronic systems. By grasping the principles of voltage, current, and resistance, future tech leaders will be better equipped to innovate and solve problems in the ever-evolving field of electronics. As you progress in your studies and careers, a strong understanding of Ohm's Law will serve as a valuable tool for navigating the complexities of the electronic landscape.

Power and Energy in Electrical Circuits

Power and energy are fundamental concepts in electrical circuits, playing a crucial role in how electronic devices function. Power, defined as the rate at which energy is transferred or converted, is measured in watts (W). In electrical circuits, power can be calculated using the formula $P = V \times I$, where P is power, V is voltage, and I is current. Understanding this relationship is essential for anyone working with electronics, as it allows for the design and analysis of circuits with adequate power supply and energy efficiency.

Energy, on the other hand, refers to the capacity to do work and is measured in joules (J). In the context of electrical circuits, energy consumption can be understood as the product of power and time, expressed in the equation $E = P \times t$, where E is energy, P is power, and t is time in seconds. This relationship highlights the importance of considering both power ratings and operational time when evaluating the total energy consumption of an electronic device. Efficient energy management is crucial for minimizing costs and environmental impact in today's technology-driven world.

In practical applications, it is vital to consider how power and energy interact within circuits. For instance, resistive components, such as resistors, dissipate energy in the form of heat, which affects the overall efficiency of a circuit. Conversely, reactive components, like capacitors and inductors, store and release energy, leading to different dynamics in power consumption. Understanding these behaviors is essential for designing circuits that not only meet performance requirements but also operate efficiently under varying loads and conditions.

Moreover, the role of power supply in circuits cannot be underestimated. Power supplies convert electrical energy from one form to another, ensuring that the voltage and current levels are appropriate for the components used in a circuit. Choosing the right power supply is critical, as it directly influences the performance and reliability of electronic devices. Additionally, modern power management techniques, such as switching regulators and linear power supplies, are designed to enhance energy efficiency, providing a pathway for more sustainable electronic designs.

Finally, for future tech leaders and engineers, grasping the concepts of power and energy in electrical circuits is vital for innovation. As technologies evolve, the demand for energy-efficient and high-performance devices continues to grow. Mastery of these principles not only equips students and professionals with the necessary skills to tackle current challenges but also positions them to drive advancements in sustainable technology. Embracing this knowledge is a stepping stone toward developing the next generation of electronic products that prioritize both functionality and energy efficiency.

CHAPTER 3

COMPONENTS OF ELECTRONIC CIRCUITS

Resistors

Resistors are fundamental components in electronic circuits, serving a crucial role in controlling the flow of electric current. They are designed to limit current, divide voltages, and dissipate power in the form of heat. The basic principle underlying resistors is Ohm's Law, which states that the current flowing through a conductor between two points is directly proportional to the voltage across the two points and inversely proportional to the resistance. This relationship is essential for understanding circuit behavior and is a cornerstone of electronics.

Resistors come in various types, each suited for specific applications. The most common types include carbon composition, film, wirewound, and surface mount resistors. Carbon composition resistors are often used in applications where high energy pulses occur, while film resistors provide better precision and stability. Wirewound resistors, made by winding a metal wire around a ceramic core, can handle higher power levels but are larger in size. Surface mount resistors are compact and suitable for modern electronics, allowing for high-density circuit designs. Understanding the characteristics and applications of these resistor types is vital for any aspiring tech leader.

The value of a resistor is measured in ohms, and resistors are often color-coded to indicate their resistance value and tolerance. The color bands provide a quick reference for identifying these specifications. Tolerance indicates how much the actual resistance can vary from the nominal value, which is critical when precision is required in circuits. In practical applications, engineers often use resistors in voltage dividers, pull-up and pull-down configurations, and biasing transistors. These configurations are essential for ensuring that devices operate within their intended parameters.

Power rating is another important aspect of resistors. It defines the maximum amount of power a resistor can dissipate without being damaged, typically expressed in watts. Exceeding this rating can lead to overheating and potential failure. Engineers must consider both the resistance value and the power rating when selecting resistors for specific applications to ensure reliability and performance. Proper thermal management is also essential, as excessive heat can degrade resistor performance over time.

In conclusion, resistors are indispensable components in the field of electronics, playing a vital role in both simple and complex circuits. Their ability to control current and voltage makes them a necessary building block for any electronic device. As technology continues to advance, understanding the intricacies of resistors will empower future tech leaders to design more efficient and innovative electronic systems. Mastery of resistor applications and characteristics will pave the way for successful ventures in engineering and technology.

Capacitors

Capacitors are fundamental components in electronic circuits, essential for storing and releasing electrical energy. These passive devices consist of two conductive plates separated by an insulating material known as a dielectric. The ability of a capacitor to store charge is quantified by its capacitance, measured in farads (F). Capacitance is directly proportional to the surface area of the plates and inversely proportional to the distance between them. This relationship highlights how the design and material selection of capacitors can significantly affect their performance in various applications.

There are several types of capacitors, each with unique characteristics suited for specific applications. Ceramic capacitors are popular for their stability and reliability, making them ideal for high-frequency applications. Electrolytic capacitors, on the other hand, are often used in power supply circuits due to their high capacitance values and ability to handle larger voltage levels. Tantalum capacitors offer a compact size and excellent performance but can be more expensive. Understanding the differences between these capacitor types allows engineers and tech founders to make informed decisions when designing circuits.

Capacitors play a critical role in filtering applications, where they smooth out voltage fluctuations in power supplies. In a typical circuit, capacitors can eliminate noise and ripple in DC voltage, ensuring that the output remains stable. This is particularly important in sensitive electronic devices where consistent power is crucial. Additionally, capacitors are used in timing applications, where they work in conjunction with resistors to create delays or oscillations, forming the basis for timing circuits found in microcontrollers and other digital devices.

In signal processing, capacitors are vital for coupling and decoupling signals between different stages of an electronic circuit. Coupling capacitors allow AC signals to pass while blocking DC components, enabling effective transmission of audio and radio frequency signals. Decoupling capacitors are employed to stabilize power supply voltages by providing a local reservoir of charge, thus reducing noise and improving the performance of sensitive components. These functions underscore the versatility of capacitors in enhancing circuit performance across various domains.

As technology continues to evolve, the role of capacitors is becoming increasingly significant, especially with the rise of renewable energy systems and electric vehicles. Advanced capacitor technologies, such as supercapacitors, are being developed to meet the demand for energy storage solutions that bridge the gap between traditional capacitors and batteries. These innovations present exciting opportunities for computer students, engineers, and tech founders to explore new applications and drive advancements in electronic design. Understanding the principles and applications of capacitors will empower the next generation of tech leaders to harness their potential effectively.

Inductors

Inductors are fundamental components in the realm of electronics, playing a crucial role in the behavior of electrical circuits. They consist of a coil of wire wound around a core, which can be air, iron, or other magnetic materials. When an electric current flows through the coil, a magnetic field is generated around it. This magnetic field is essential for the inductor's function, as it allows the component to store energy temporarily. The ability to store energy distinguishes inductors from resistors and capacitors, making them indispensable in various applications, including power supplies, filters, and oscillators.

One of the defining characteristics of inductors is their inductance, measured in henries (H). Inductance quantifies the inductor's ability to store energy in its magnetic field, and it depends on several factors, including the number of turns in the coil, the material of the core, and the coil's geometry. The relationship between the current flowing through the inductor and the voltage across it is governed by Faraday's law of electromagnetic induction. When the current through the inductor changes, the magnetic field also changes, inducing a voltage that opposes the current change. This behavior is described by Lenz's Law, highlighting the inductor's ability to resist changes in current.

Inductors find widespread use in various electronic circuits. In power supplies, they are often employed in conjunction with capacitors to filter and smooth out voltage fluctuations. This combination creates a low-pass filter, allowing only certain frequencies to pass while attenuating others. Additionally, in radio frequency applications, inductors are crucial for tuning circuits, enabling the selection of specific frequencies for transmission and reception. Their role in energy storage also makes them vital in switch-mode power supplies, where they help manage energy transfer efficiently.

The construction of inductors can vary significantly depending on their intended application. Air-core inductors are typically used in high-frequency applications due to their lower losses, while iron-core inductors offer higher inductance values at lower frequencies but may suffer from core losses due to hysteresis and eddy currents. Additionally, toroidal inductors, shaped like a doughnut, are favored for their compact size and reduced electromagnetic interference. Choosing the right type of inductor for a specific application involves considering factors such as inductance value, current rating, and frequency response.

Understanding the behavior and applications of inductors is essential for anyone involved in electronics, from students to tech founders. As technology continues to evolve, the demand for efficient energy management solutions grows. Inductors will remain integral to circuit design, enabling innovations in power electronics, communications, and various other fields. By mastering the principles of inductors, aspiring engineers and tech leaders can develop the skills necessary to design and implement cutting-edge electronic systems that meet the challenges of tomorrow's technology landscape.

Diodes

Diodes are fundamental electronic components that play a crucial role in circuits by controlling the direction of current flow. At their core, diodes are semiconductor devices that allow current to pass in one direction while blocking it in the opposite direction. This property makes them essential in various applications, including rectification, signal modulation, and voltage regulation. Understanding diodes is vital for anyone entering the fields of computer science, engineering, or technology entrepreneurship, as they form the backbone of many electronic systems.

The most common type of diode is the silicon diode, which consists of a p-n junction formed by joining p-type and n-type semiconductor materials. When forward biased, meaning the positive voltage is applied to the p-side, the diode conducts current. Conversely, when reverse biased, with the positive voltage applied to the n-side, the diode prevents current flow. This unidirectional behavior is exploited in power supplies to convert alternating current (AC) to direct current (DC), highlighting the diode's role in ensuring devices receive the correct type of power.

Another important category of diodes is the Zener diode, which is designed to allow current to flow in the reverse direction when a specific voltage, known as the Zener breakdown voltage, is reached. Zener diodes are widely used for voltage regulation within circuits, providing a stable output voltage regardless of variations in input voltage or load conditions. Their ability to maintain a constant voltage makes them invaluable in power supply circuits and in protecting sensitive components from voltage spikes.

Light-emitting diodes (LEDs) represent a specialized type of diode that emits light when current flows through them. LEDs are highly efficient and have become ubiquitous in modern electronics, serving as indicators, displays, and even sources of illumination. Their low power consumption and long lifespan have led to their widespread adoption in various applications, from consumer electronics to automotive lighting. Understanding the functionality of LEDs and their driving requirements is crucial for tech founders looking to innovate in lighting and display technologies.

Finally, the invention of Schottky diodes has further expanded the capabilities of diodes in electronic applications. Schottky diodes are known for their low forward voltage drop and fast switching speeds, making them ideal for high-frequency applications such as power rectification in switch-mode power supplies. Their unique characteristics allow for more efficient designs, reducing energy losses and improving overall circuit performance. As technology continues to advance, the fundamental principles of diodes will remain integral to the development of new electronic systems and innovations.

Transistors

Transistors are fundamental components in modern electronics, serving as the building blocks for a wide array of devices, from simple amplifiers to complex microprocessors. A transistor is a semiconductor device that can both amplify and switch electronic signals and electrical power. Their ability to control current flow makes them essential for numerous applications in electronic circuits. Transistors operate primarily by controlling the flow of charge carriers in a semiconductor material, typically silicon, which has revolutionized the way electronic devices function since their invention in the mid-20th century.

There are three main types of transistors: bipolar junction transistors (BJTs), field-effect transistors (FETs), and insulated-gate bipolar transistors (IGBTs). BJTs are current-controlled devices that utilize both electron and hole charge carriers, while FETs are voltage-controlled devices that rely on an electric field to control the flow of current. IGBTs combine the advantages of both BJTs and FETs, making them suitable for high-voltage and high-current applications. Understanding the differences between these types is crucial for engineers and tech founders, as each type has specific use cases and performance characteristics that can influence the design and functionality of electronic systems.

Transistors are typically used in two primary configurations:

common emitter and common source for BJTs and FETs, respectively. In a common emitter configuration, the input signal is applied to the base of the BJT, and the output is taken from the collector, allowing for significant amplification of the input signal. Similarly, in a common source configuration for FETs, the input signal is applied to the gate, and the output is drawn from the drain. These configurations demonstrate how transistors can manipulate signals, making them essential in applications such as signal processing, switching, and amplification in various electronic devices.

The miniaturization of transistors has led to the development of integrated circuits (ICs), which contain thousands to millions of transistors on a single chip. This advancement has allowed for the creation of powerful microprocessors and memory chips, enabling the performance of modern computers and smartphones. The transition from discrete components to integrated circuits represents a significant leap in technology, allowing for more compact, efficient, and reliable electronic systems. As computer students and engineering professionals explore circuit design, understanding the role of transistors in ICs will be critical for developing innovative tech solutions.

Future advancements in transistor technology, including the exploration of new materials such as graphene and advances in quantum computing, promise to further enhance performance and efficiency. As the demand for faster, smaller, and more energy-efficient devices continues to grow, ongoing research in transistor design and manufacturing will play a crucial role in shaping the future of electronics. For tech founders and engineering students, keeping abreast of these developments will not only enhance their understanding but also prepare them to contribute to the next generation of electronic innovations.

CHAPTER 4

CIRCUIT DESIGN AND ANALYSIS

Understanding Circuit Diagrams

Understanding circuit diagrams is essential for anyone entering the fields of electronics, computer engineering, or technology entrepreneurship. These diagrams serve as a visual representation of electrical circuits, illustrating how components are interconnected. By deciphering these illustrations, students and professionals can gain insights into the functionality of complex systems, troubleshoot problems, and communicate ideas effectively. Being proficient in reading and interpreting circuit diagrams is a fundamental skill that lays the groundwork for more advanced studies in electronics and circuit design.

A circuit diagram typically consists of symbols that represent various electronic components such as resistors, capacitors, diodes, and transistors. Each symbol conveys specific information about the component's function and characteristics. For instance, a resistor is depicted as a zigzag line, while a capacitor is shown as two parallel lines. Understanding these

symbols is crucial, as they form the language of circuit diagrams. Familiarity with the standard symbols allows students to quickly grasp the layout and function of a circuit, facilitating easier analysis and design.

The arrangement of components in a circuit diagram is not arbitrary; it reflects the flow of electricity through the system. Lines connecting the symbols represent electrical connections, while the layout indicates how components interact with one another. This spatial arrangement helps in understanding the overall operation of a circuit. For example, a series circuit will show components connected end-to-end, while a parallel circuit will have branches that diverge from a common connection point. Recognizing these configurations is vital for diagnosing issues, predicting circuit behavior, and implementing effective solutions in practical applications.

Moreover, circuit diagrams can vary in complexity, from simple designs for basic electronic projects to intricate schematics for advanced systems. Beginners may start with straightforward diagrams that involve a few components, gradually progressing to more complicated architectures as their skills improve. Each step in this progression reinforces the understanding of fundamental principles such as Ohm's Law and Kirchhoff's Laws. By tackling increasingly complex diagrams, students can cultivate their analytical abilities and confidence in working with electronic circuits.

In conclusion, mastering circuit diagrams is a critical step for anyone aspiring to excel in electronics, engineering, or technology entrepreneurship. This skill not only enhances technical knowledge but also fosters effective communication among peers and stakeholders in the field. As students engage with various circuit diagrams, they develop a deeper appreciation for the intricacies of electronic systems and prepare themselves for the challenges of tomorrow's technological landscape. Embracing this foundational knowledge will empower future tech leaders to innovate and contribute meaningfully to their chosen domains.

Series and Parallel Circuits

In electronics, understanding the configuration of circuits is fundamental for anyone looking to delve into the world of technology. Two primary configurations exist: series and parallel circuits. Each configuration has distinct characteristics, advantages, and disadvantages that play crucial roles in determining how components interact within a circuit. Comprehending these differences is essential for computer students, engineers, and tech founders as they design and troubleshoot electronic systems.

In a series circuit, components are connected end-to-end, forming a single path for current to flow. This configuration means that the same current flows through each component, which can lead to predictable behavior in terms of voltage drops across each device. For example, if a series circuit contains three resistors, the total resistance is the sum of the individual resistances. This characteristic can be advantageous in applications where a uniform current is required, but it can also lead to challenges. If one component fails or is disconnected, the entire circuit is interrupted, rendering all components inoperative.

Conversely, a parallel circuit connects components across common points or junctions, allowing multiple pathways for current to flow. In this configuration, each component operates independently; if one component fails, the others continue to function. The total resistance in a parallel circuit is calculated using a different formula, resulting in a lower overall resistance compared to any individual component. This makes parallel circuits particularly useful in applications where reliability is crucial, such as in household wiring and electronic devices, where multiple components must operate simultaneously without interruption.

The choice between series and parallel circuits often depends on the specific requirements of the application. Series circuits might be preferred in situations where simplicity and space-saving are paramount, such as in string lights or basic sensor circuits. On the other hand, parallel circuits are favored in scenarios that require redundancy and reliability, such as in computer power supplies and automotive wiring systems. Understanding these contexts allows future tech leaders to make informed decisions regarding circuit design and implementation based on operational needs.

Ultimately, mastering the concepts of series and parallel circuits is a stepping stone for budding engineers and tech innovators. These fundamental principles not only shape the way electronic devices are constructed but also influence how they are maintained and repaired. As technology continues to evolve, a solid grasp of these circuit configurations will empower future leaders in the tech industry to innovate and solve complex problems efficiently.

Analyzing Circuit Behavior

Analyzing circuit behavior is essential for understanding how electronic components interact within a system. This process involves using both theoretical principles and practical tools to interpret the performance of circuits under various conditions. By dissecting circuit behavior, students and future tech leaders can identify potential issues, optimize designs, and innovate solutions. The foundation of this analysis lies in understanding voltage, current, resistance, and the relationships between these elements as defined by Ohm's Law and Kirchhoff's Laws.

One fundamental aspect of circuit behavior analysis is the use of circuit simulation software. Tools such as SPICE (Simulation Program with Integrated Circuit Emphasis) allow users to model circuits without physically building them. This capability is invaluable for testing hypotheses and exploring circuit designs. By inputting various parameters, students can observe how changes affect performance, enabling them to make informed decisions before committing to hardware. Simulations also facilitate learning by allowing real-time adjustments and visualizations of circuit responses.

In addition to simulations, practical measurements play a critical role in analyzing circuit behavior. Instruments such as oscilloscopes, multimeters, and function generators provide insight into real-world performance. By measuring voltage and current at different points in a circuit, students can evaluate whether the circuit behaves as expected. This hands-on experience reinforces theoretical knowledge and helps identify discrepancies that may arise due to component tolerances, temperature variations, or unanticipated interactions between components.

Another important consideration in circuit behavior analysis is the frequency response of circuits, especially in alternating current (AC) applications. Understanding how resistors, capacitors, and inductors react to different frequencies is crucial for designing efficient circuits, particularly in communication devices and signal processing systems. Analyzing frequency response involves techniques such as Bode plots, which graphically represent how gain and phase shift vary with frequency. This analysis aids in selecting appropriate components and configurations to meet specific performance criteria.

Lastly, analyzing circuit behavior extends beyond individual components and encompasses the entire system's response. This holistic view is essential for complex designs, where the interaction between many components can lead to non-linear behaviors. Techniques such as network analysis and feedback system analysis help in understanding how changes in one part of the circuit can influence overall performance. By mastering these analytical techniques, students and tech leaders will be better equipped to design innovative solutions that push the boundaries of electronic technology.

Introduction to Circuit Simulation Tools

Circuit simulation tools are essential in the realm of electronics, providing a virtual environment for designing, analyzing, and testing electronic circuits. These tools allow users to visualize how circuits behave under various conditions without the need for physical components, which can be costly and time-consuming to assemble. By simulating circuits, engineers and students can experiment with different configurations, components, and parameters, gaining insights into their designs before committing to hardware. This not only enhances understanding but also fosters innovation by allowing users to explore unconventional ideas without the risk of damaging real components.

One of the primary advantages of circuit simulation tools is their ability to model complex interactions within circuits. Many modern simulation programs offer advanced features such as transient analysis, frequency response analysis, and Monte Carlo simulations. These capabilities enable users to assess how circuits will perform over time, in response to different signals, or under varying environmental conditions. For students and future tech leaders, mastering these tools is crucial, as they provide the foundation for understanding more intricate electronic systems and design methodologies.

The market offers a range of circuit simulation tools, from free, open-source options to professional-grade software. Popular tools such as LTspice, Multisim, and PSpice cater to different user needs and levels of complexity. While some tools focus on ease of use, making them ideal for beginners, others provide extensive libraries of components and advanced analysis features that benefit seasoned professionals. Understanding the strengths and limitations of various simulation tools can help users select the most appropriate software for their specific projects and learning objectives.

Integrating circuit simulation into educational curricula enhances the learning experience for students in electronics and engineering. It allows them to apply theoretical concepts in a practical setting, bridging the gap between classroom learning and real-world applications. Students can engage in hands-on projects, troubleshoot designs, and collaborate with peers, all within a simulated environment. This experiential learning process is particularly beneficial in fostering critical thinking and problem-solving skills, essential attributes for future tech leaders.

As technology continues to evolve, the importance of circuit simulation tools will only grow. The increasing complexity of electronic systems, driven by advancements in fields such as IoT, AI, and renewable energy, necessitates a deeper understanding of circuit behavior. By leveraging these tools, aspiring engineers and tech entrepreneurs will be better equipped to tackle the challenges of modern electronics design. Embracing circuit simulation not only enhances technical proficiency but also cultivates a mindset geared towards innovation and continuous learning, essential traits in today's fast-paced technological landscape.

CHAPTER 5

INTRODUCTION TO ANALOG ELECTRONICS

Amplifiers and Their Applications

Amplifiers are fundamental components in electronics that serve to increase the amplitude of a signal without significantly altering its other characteristics. They are vital in various applications ranging from audio equipment to communication systems. Understanding how amplifiers function and their different types is crucial for computer students, engineers, and tech founders who aim to innovate in the tech landscape. The basic principle behind an amplifier is the ability to take a small input signal and produce a larger output signal, making them essential in scenarios where signal strength needs to be enhanced for effective processing or transmission.

There are several types of amplifiers, each designed for specific applications. The most common types include operational amplifiers, audio amplifiers, and radio frequency amplifiers. Operational amplifiers are versatile and used in various applications such as signal conditioning, filtering, and mathematical operations. Audio amplifiers, on the other hand, are designed specifically for boosting audio signals to drive speakers, ensuring high fidelity and clear sound reproduction. Radio frequency amplifiers are crucial in communication technologies, as they enhance signals in the radio frequency spectrum, allowing for clearer transmissions over long distances.

In practical applications, amplifiers are used in numerous devices that students and engineers frequently encounter. For instance, in smartphones, amplifiers are utilized to enhance both the audio output and the signals received from cellular networks. Similarly, in medical devices, amplifiers play a critical role in interpreting signals from sensors, ensuring accurate readings in diagnostic equipment. This versatility demonstrates the integral role amplifiers play in modern technology and their importance in the development of innovative solutions across various fields.

Moreover, the design and implementation of amplifiers present unique challenges and opportunities for tech founders. Understanding the parameters such as gain, bandwidth, and input/output impedance is crucial for optimizing performance. Founders can leverage this knowledge to create new products that push the boundaries of existing technology. For example, advancements in amplifier technology could lead to more efficient audio systems or improved communication devices, highlighting the potential for innovation grounded in a solid understanding of these electronic components.

In conclusion, amplifiers are more than just components; they are the building blocks of many electronic systems that have shaped the way we communicate, interact, and experience technology. For computer students, engineers, and tech founders, a thorough comprehension of amplifiers and their applications opens the door to a multitude of opportunities in the tech industry. As technology continues to evolve, the ongoing exploration of amplifiers will remain a critical area of study and innovation, paving the way for the next generation of electronic solutions.

Oscillators and Signal Generators

Oscillators and signal generators are essential components in the field of electronics, providing the foundation for various applications ranging from communication systems to signal processing. An oscillator is a circuit that produces a continuous waveform, typically in the form of a sine, square, or triangle wave. These devices convert direct current (DC) from a power supply into an alternating current (AC) signal, which can be utilized for numerous functions, including clock signals in digital circuits, audio signal generation, and frequency modulation.

Understanding the principles and types of oscillators is crucial for anyone aspiring to innovate in technology.

There are several types of oscillators, each designed for specific applications and operating principles. Common types include the RC oscillator, LC oscillator, and crystal oscillator. RC oscillators utilize a resistor-capacitor network to set the frequency of oscillation, making them simple and cost-effective for low-frequency applications. In contrast, LC oscillators use inductors and capacitors to achieve higher frequencies and are often found in radio frequency applications. Crystal oscillators, known for their exceptional frequency stability, rely on the mechanical resonance of a vibrating crystal to produce precise frequencies, making them ubiquitous in microprocessors and communication devices.

Signal generators, closely related to oscillators, are versatile instruments used to create electrical signals for testing and analysis purposes. They can produce a range of waveforms, including sine, square, triangle, and pulse signals, and are often employed in laboratories and manufacturing processes to test electronic equipment. Signal generators can vary in complexity from simple function generators to sophisticated arbitrary waveform generators that allow users to create custom waveforms. This capability is particularly valuable for engineers and technologists who need to simulate real-world conditions for troubleshooting and calibration.

The practical applications of oscillators and signal generators extend to various fields, including telecommunications, audio engineering, and instrumentation. In telecommunications, oscillators are integral to modulating and demodulating signals, facilitating the transmission of data over long distances. In audio engineering, they generate tones and control the pitch in synthesizers and sound effects. Furthermore, in instrumentation, signal generators aid in the calibration of devices by providing known signals for measurement and analysis, ensuring accuracy and reliability in electronic systems.

In conclusion, a solid understanding of oscillators and signal generators is vital for aspiring tech leaders and engineers. These components not only form the backbone of many electronic systems but also play a critical role in the development and testing of new technologies. As advancements in electronics continue to evolve, mastering these fundamental building blocks will empower future innovators to create more efficient, reliable, and cutting-edge solutions in the tech landscape.

Filters and Frequency Response

Filters are essential components in electronic systems, designed to allow certain frequencies to pass while attenuating others. This capability is critical in a variety of applications, from audio processing to communication systems. Filters can be categorized into several types based on their frequency response characteristics: low-pass, high-pass, band-pass, and band-stop filters. Each type serves a specific purpose, allowing engineers and tech leaders to manipulate signals effectively. Understanding the principles behind these filters is fundamental for anyone involved in electronics, as they provide the foundational knowledge necessary for designing and implementing complex systems.

The frequency response of a filter characterizes how it behaves across different frequencies. This response is typically represented graphically, showing how the output amplitude varies with frequency. Key parameters include cutoff frequency, which defines the threshold at which the filter begins to attenuate the signal, and the roll-off rate, indicating how quickly the filter reduces the signal strength beyond the cutoff. Additionally, filters may exhibit different behaviors in terms of phase shift, which affects the timing of the output signal relative to the input. A deep understanding of frequency response allows engineers to select or design filters that meet the specific requirements of their applications.

Active filters, which utilize operational amplifiers and other active components, offer improved performance over passive filters. They can provide gain, have a more selective frequency response, and can be designed to have a more complex behavior without the size and power limitations of passive components. This flexibility makes active filters particularly valuable in modern electronic systems, where size and efficiency are paramount. Engineers must consider the trade-offs between active and passive filters based on the application's requirements, including factors such as power consumption, linearity, and component availability.

Digital filters have gained prominence in recent years due to advancements in digital signal processing (DSP). These filters allow for precise control over the filtering process and can implement complex algorithms for signal manipulation. Digital filters operate through algorithms that process sampled signals, which can lead to improved performance in terms of noise reduction and signal fidelity. Understanding the basics of digital filtering techniques, such as Finite Impulse Response (FIR) and Infinite Impulse Response (IIR), empowers tech leaders to leverage modern computing capabilities for innovative solutions in electronics.

Ultimately, the design and application of filters and their frequency response are critical skills for future tech leaders. As technology continues to evolve, the ability to manipulate and control signals effectively will play a significant role in the development of new electronic devices and systems. By mastering the concepts surrounding filters, engineers can ensure optimal performance in various applications, paving the way for advancements in fields such as telecommunications, audio engineering, and beyond. Embracing these principles will equip the next generation of tech innovators with the tools they need to tackle complex challenges in the electronic landscape.

CHAPTER 6

DIGITAL ELECTRONICS FUNDAMENTALS

Binary Number System

The binary number system is a fundamental concept in electronics and computer science, serving as the backbone of modern computing technology. Unlike the decimal system, which uses ten digits (0-9), the binary system employs only two digits: 0 and 1. Each digit in a binary number is referred to as a bit, and the arrangement of these bits allows for the representation of any numerical value or character. This simplicity is crucial for electronic devices, as it aligns seamlessly with the on-off states of electrical circuits, where 1 represents an 'on' state and 0 represents an 'off' state.

In binary, each position in a number represents a power of two, rather than a power of ten as in the decimal system. For example, the binary number 1011 can be broken down into its component parts: 1 in the 2^3 position, 0 in the 2^2 position, 1 in the 2^1 position, and 1 in the 2^0 position. When these values are calculated, 1011 in binary equals 11 in decimal (1*8 + 0*4 + 1*2 + 1*1). This method of understanding binary numbers is essential for students and professionals alike, as it forms the basis for more complex operations in programming and digital electronics.

Binary numbers are not only used for arithmetic calculations but also play a vital role in data representation. In computers, all forms of data—whether text, images, or sound—are ultimately converted into binary form. Each character or pixel corresponds to a specific binary sequence, allowing for efficient storage and processing. For instance, the ASCII encoding system represents characters using a unique 7 or 8-bit binary code, enabling computers to handle text data effectively. Understanding these representations is crucial for aspiring tech leaders who aim to innovate in software development and data management.

The importance of the binary system extends to its application in logic gates and circuits, which are the building blocks of digital systems. Logic gates use binary inputs to produce a binary output based on predefined logical operations such as AND, OR, and NOT. These gates form the basis of more complex computational operations, allowing for decision-making processes within circuits. Mastery of binary logic is essential for engineers and tech founders who seek to design efficient and powerful electronic systems capable of processing vast amounts of data.

In conclusion, the binary number system is not just an abstract mathematical concept but a practical tool that underpins the functionality of electronic devices and computer systems. Its simplicity and efficiency make it an ideal choice for digital representation, while its integration into logic circuits allows for advanced computing capabilities. For students and professionals in the tech field, a strong grasp of binary principles is imperative for navigating the ever-evolving landscape of technology and engineering, positioning them to contribute effectively to innovative solutions in the future.

Logic Gates and Boolean Algebra

Logic gates are fundamental building blocks in digital electronics, serving as the primary means of performing logical operations on binary data. Each gate corresponds to a specific logical operation, namely AND, OR, NOT, NAND, NOR, XOR, and XNOR. These gates can be implemented using various technologies, including transistors, diodes, and integrated circuits. Understanding the behavior and functionality of these gates is crucial for anyone involved in computer science or engineering, as they form the basis for more complex systems such as microprocessors and memory devices.

Boolean algebra is the mathematical framework that underpins the operation of logic gates. Developed by George Boole in the mid-19th century, Boolean algebra allows for the manipulation of binary variables using a set of axioms and rules. In this algebra, variables can take on values of either 0 (false) or 1 (true), and operations such as AND, OR, and NOT are represented by specific mathematical symbols. By applying Boolean algebra, engineers can simplify logic expressions, optimize circuit design, and predict the behavior of digital systems.

The interplay between logic gates and Boolean algebra becomes evident in the design and analysis of digital circuits. For instance, a combination of multiple gates can be used to implement complex functions. By using truth tables, engineers can visualize the relationships between inputs and outputs, facilitating the abstraction of circuit designs into manageable components. This process often involves reducing expressions using Boolean identities, which can lead to more efficient circuits with fewer components, ultimately saving space and power.

In practical applications, the knowledge of logic gates and Boolean algebra is indispensable in areas such as computer architecture, digital signal processing, and embedded systems. For computer students and aspiring tech founders, mastering these concepts enables them to design robust hardware and software solutions. Whether developing algorithms or creating circuit designs, understanding how to manipulate binary data through logic gates is a skill that will enhance their capability to innovate in technology.

As technology continues to evolve, the importance of logic gates and Boolean algebra remains steadfast. With the rise of quantum computing and advanced digital systems, these foundational concepts will serve as a springboard for future innovations. By grasping the principles of logic gates and Boolean algebra, students and engineers position themselves at the forefront of technological advancements, equipped to tackle the challenges of tomorrow's electronic landscape.

Combinational and Sequential Logic Circuits

Combinational and sequential logic circuits are fundamental components in the realm of digital electronics, serving as the building blocks for more complex systems. Combinational logic circuits are designed to produce outputs based solely on the current inputs without any memory of past inputs. This means that the output is a direct function of the present input values. Common examples include basic gates such as AND, OR, and NOT, which can be combined to create more complex functions. These circuits can be analyzed and designed using truth tables, Boolean algebra, and Karnaugh maps, allowing engineers to simplify the logic and optimize circuit performance.

In contrast, sequential logic circuits incorporate memory elements, meaning their outputs depend not only on the current inputs but also on past inputs. This characteristic enables sequential circuits to store information, making them essential for applications requiring data retention. Flip-flops, latches, and registers are typical components of sequential logic circuits. They are utilized in various applications, including counters, shift registers, and finite state machines, where the order of operations and timing are crucial. Understanding the differences between combinational and sequential circuits is vital for designing effective digital systems.

The design process for combinational logic circuits typically begins with defining the desired outputs based on specific input conditions. Engineers employ tools like truth tables and Boolean expressions to determine how to connect various logic gates. Once the logic has been established, it is essential to analyze the circuit for potential optimizations, such as reducing the number of gates used or minimizing propagation delays. Simulation software can be invaluable during this phase, allowing designers to visualize circuit behavior under different conditions and troubleshoot issues before physical implementation.

Sequential logic design, on the other hand, involves a more complex approach due to the need for timing considerations and state representation. Engineers often create state diagrams to represent the various conditions of the circuit and the transitions between states. Synchronous sequential circuits operate based on clock signals, ensuring that state changes occur at specific intervals, while asynchronous circuits respond immediately to input changes. The choice of synchronization method can significantly influence the performance, reliability, and complexity of the final design.

Understanding both combinational and sequential logic circuits is essential for anyone aspiring to lead in the tech field. Mastery of these concepts equips future engineers and tech founders with the skills necessary to develop innovative electronic systems. As technology evolves, the integration of these circuits into more complex architectures highlights the importance of a solid foundation in digital logic. This knowledge not only fosters creativity but also enhances problem-solving capabilities, enabling the creation of efficient, reliable, and cutting-edge electronic devices.

CHAPTER 7

MICROCONTROLLERS AND MICROPROCESSORS

Overview of Microcontrollers

Microcontrollers are compact integrated circuits designed to govern specific operations in embedded systems. They combine a microprocessor core with programmable memory and various input/output peripherals. Unlike general-purpose processors used in personal computers, microcontrollers are tailored for specific tasks, making them ideal for applications ranging from household appliances to sophisticated automotive systems. Their ability to execute predefined tasks efficiently and reliably is what makes them fundamental in the realm of electronics and automation.

The architecture of a microcontroller typically includes a central processing unit (CPU), memory (both read-only memory and random access memory), and input/output ports. The CPU processes instructions from the program stored in memory, while the input/output ports facilitate communication with other devices or sensors. This architecture allows microcontrollers to interact with the external environment, making them versatile components in various electronic applications. Understanding this architecture is crucial for students and tech founders as it lays the groundwork for designing and implementing embedded systems.

Programming microcontrollers involves using different languages, with C and assembly language being the most prevalent. These languages allow engineers to write instructions that the microcontroller will execute. The choice of language often depends on the complexity of the task and the specific microcontroller being used. Students and aspiring tech leaders should familiarize themselves with programming concepts and tools, as this knowledge will enable them to create more sophisticated and efficient applications. Moreover, a solid understanding of programming can lead to innovative solutions in various fields, including robotics, automation, and the Internet of Things (IoT).

Microcontrollers have evolved significantly over the years, with manufacturers continuously improving their capabilities. Modern microcontrollers often incorporate features such as higher processing speeds, more extensive memory, and advanced peripherals like analog-to-digital converters and communication interfaces. These enhancements expand their application range, allowing them to perform complex functions and interface with other devices seamlessly. For engineering students and tech founders, staying abreast of these advancements is essential for leveraging the latest technology in their projects and products.

The impact of microcontrollers on the electronics industry is profound. They have revolutionized the design and functionality of countless devices, driving innovation across various sectors. From consumer electronics to industrial automation, microcontrollers enable the development of smarter, more efficient systems. For computer students and engineering professionals, understanding microcontrollers is not just about mastering a component; it's about grasping the foundational elements that drive the future of technology. As industries continue to evolve toward greater automation and connectivity, the relevance of microcontrollers in shaping the future of electronics will only increase.

Programming Microcontrollers

Programming microcontrollers is a fundamental skill for anyone interested in electronics and embedded systems. Microcontrollers serve as the brains of many devices, from household appliances to advanced robotic systems. Understanding how to program these small computers allows students and future tech leaders to create innovative solutions and bring their ideas to life. The process generally involves writing code in a high-level programming language, compiling it into machine code, and uploading it to the microcontroller for execution.

The first step in programming microcontrollers is selecting the right platform. Popular options include Arduino, Raspberry Pi, and various microcontroller families such as PIC and AVR. Each platform has its own architecture, programming environment, and community support. Arduino, for instance, is known for its user-friendly interface and extensive library support, making it an excellent choice for beginners. As students explore different platforms, they should consider factors like ease of use, available resources, and the specific requirements of their projects.

Once a platform is chosen, the next step is to understand the programming languages commonly used. C and C++ are among the most popular languages for microcontroller programming due to their efficiency and control over hardware. Additionally, some platforms support other languages, such as Python or JavaScript, which can simplify the programming process for those already familiar with them. Students should familiarize themselves with the syntax and structure of these languages, as well as concepts like data types, control structures, and functions, which are essential for writing effective code.

In addition to coding, students must learn about interfacing microcontrollers with various components and sensors. This involves understanding how to read inputs from sensors, control outputs like motors or LEDs, and communicate with other devices through protocols such as I2C, SPI, or UART. Effective programming requires a solid grasp of both hardware and software, as well as the ability to troubleshoot issues that may arise during the development process. Practical experience through projects and experiments will reinforce these concepts and build confidence in handling real-world applications.

Finally, as students develop their programming skills, they should also explore the importance of debugging and optimization. Debugging involves identifying and fixing errors in the code, which can be achieved through tools like simulators or built-in debugging features of development environments. Optimization focuses on enhancing the performance of the code, such as reducing memory usage or improving execution speed. By mastering these techniques, future tech leaders will be better equipped to create efficient, reliable systems that can handle the complexities of modern technology.

Applications of Microcontrollers in Modern Electronics

Microcontrollers serve as the backbone of modern electronics, enabling a wide range of applications that are integral to today's technology landscape. These compact integrated circuits combine a processor, memory, and input/output peripherals on a single chip, allowing for efficient control over various devices and systems. In consumer electronics, microcontrollers are ubiquitous, found in products like smartphones, smart home devices, and wearables. Their ability to execute tasks, respond to inputs, and manage outputs makes them essential for creating user-friendly interfaces and smart functionalities in these devices.

In the realm of automation and control systems, microcontrollers play a critical role in enhancing efficiency and reliability. Industrial machines, robotics, and manufacturing processes often rely on microcontrollers to automate tasks that were traditionally performed manually. By processing sensor data and controlling actuators, microcontrollers enable precise control over machinery, leading to increased productivity and reduced operational costs. This automation is not limited to large-scale industries; small businesses can also leverage microcontrollers for custom automation solutions, enhancing their competitive edge.

Microcontrollers are central to the development of the Internet of Things (IoT), a network of interconnected devices that communicate and exchange data. In IoT applications, microcontrollers serve as the brains of smart devices, collecting data from various sensors and transmitting it to cloud platforms for analysis. This connectivity allows for real-time monitoring and control of systems ranging from smart agriculture to environmental monitoring. As IoT continues to grow, the demand for microcontrollers that can handle various communication protocols and power-efficient operations will only increase, driving innovation in this space.

In the automotive industry, microcontrollers are vital for modern vehicle functionalities. They control everything from engine management systems to advanced driver-assistance systems (ADAS). By processing data from sensors such as cameras, radar, and LiDAR, microcontrollers enable features like adaptive cruise control, lane-keeping assistance, and automatic emergency braking. As vehicles become increasingly connected and autonomous, the reliance on microcontrollers will expand, leading to more sophisticated features that enhance safety and user experience.

Education and research institutions also leverage microcontrollers as teaching tools in electronics and engineering courses. Their accessibility and versatility make them ideal for hands-on learning experiences. Students can easily experiment with programming and interfacing microcontrollers in projects ranging from simple LED blinking to complex robotics. This practical approach fosters a deeper understanding of electronics and prepares future tech leaders for careers in engineering, product development, and innovation. As technology continues to evolve, familiarity with microcontrollers will be an essential skill for students entering the electronics and tech fields.

CHAPTER 8

SENSORS AND ACTUATORS

Types of Sensors

Sensors are integral components in modern electronics, providing the means to gather data from the environment and convert it into a form that can be processed by electronic systems. The variety of sensors available today reflects the diverse applications they serve, ranging from simple temperature readings to complex environmental monitoring. Understanding the different types of sensors is crucial for computer students, engineers, and tech founders who aim to innovate in the field of electronics.

The most common category of sensors is the temperature sensor. These devices detect temperature changes and convert the information into electrical signals. Thermocouples, thermistors, and infrared sensors are among the most widely used types. Thermocouples work by measuring the voltage generated at the junction of two different metals, making them suitable for high-temperature applications. In contrast, thermistors change resistance with temperature variations, offering high sensitivity for lower temperatures. Infrared sensors, often used in non-contact applications, detect the thermal radiation emitted by objects, making them ideal for measuring surface temperatures in various industrial processes.

Another significant category is motion sensors, which are employed to detect movement in a given area. Passive infrared sensors (PIR) are commonly used in security systems and automatic lighting. They detect changes in infrared radiation caused by moving objects, particularly warm bodies like humans and animals. Ultrasonic sensors, on the other hand, use sound waves to detect the presence and distance of objects. By emitting high-frequency sound waves and measuring the time it takes for the echo to return, they can provide accurate distance measurements, making them suitable for applications such as parking assistance and robotics.

Proximity sensors are similar to motion sensors but are designed to detect the presence or absence of an object within a specified range. Capacitive sensors can detect anything from a human touch to the presence of liquids, making them versatile for various applications, including touchscreens and level sensors in tanks. Inductive sensors, which rely on electromagnetic fields, are used primarily in industrial settings to detect metallic objects. These sensors are pivotal in automation processes where the precise identification of objects is critical to operational efficiency.

Finally, environmental sensors, which monitor various aspects of the surroundings, are becoming increasingly important as technology integrates into smart cities and IoT applications. These sensors can measure air quality, humidity, light intensity, and even soil moisture levels. Gas sensors, for example, detect the presence of harmful gases and are essential for safety in industrial environments. As the demand for sustainability and environmental awareness grows, the role of these sensors in providing real-time data for informed decision-making becomes more significant, helping to improve both quality of life and resource management.

Understanding the various types of sensors and their functionalities is essential for aspiring tech leaders and engineers. As technology continues to advance, the integration of multiple sensor types will enable the development of smarter systems and devices. This knowledge not only fosters innovation but also prepares the next generation of professionals to tackle the challenges and opportunities presented by the ever-evolving landscape of electronics.

Working with Actuators

Actuators are critical components in the field of electronics and automation, converting electrical energy into physical motion. These devices play a pivotal role in various applications, ranging from robotics and manufacturing to consumer electronics and automotive systems. Understanding how to work with actuators is essential for computer students, engineers, and tech founders, as it enables them to design and implement systems that require precise control of movement. This subchapter will explore the different types of actuators, their working principles, and practical considerations when integrating them into projects.

There are several types of actuators, each suited for specific applications. The most common categories include electric, hydraulic, and pneumatic actuators. Electric actuators, such as DC motors and stepper motors, are widely used due to their simplicity and ease of control. Hydraulic actuators utilize fluid power to create motion, making them ideal for heavy-duty applications where high force is required. Pneumatic actuators operate using compressed air and are often found in systems requiring quick movements and lightweight solutions. Understanding these actuator types allows students and engineers to select the most appropriate option based on their project requirements.

When working with actuators, it is crucial to grasp their operational principles. Electric actuators generally rely on electromagnetic principles to create motion. For instance, DC motors function by passing current through a coil, generating a magnetic field that interacts with permanent magnets. Stepper motors, on the other hand, divide rotation into discrete steps, offering precise control over position and speed. Hydraulic and pneumatic actuators operate based on fluid dynamics, where pressure differentials cause movement. Familiarity with these principles enables effective troubleshooting and optimization of actuator performance in various applications.

Integrating actuators into electronic systems requires careful planning and consideration of several factors. Control mechanisms, such as microcontrollers or programmable logic controllers (PLCs), are commonly used to manage actuator operations. It is essential to develop appropriate control algorithms that account for feedback and ensure accurate positioning. Additionally, power supply requirements must be evaluated, as actuators often demand higher currents and voltages than standard electronic components. Safety considerations, such as incorporating limit switches or emergency stop mechanisms, are also vital to prevent damage to both the actuator and the overall system.

In conclusion, working with actuators is a fundamental aspect of building effective electronic systems. By understanding the various types of actuators, their operating principles, and the necessary integration techniques, computer students, engineers, and tech founders can enhance their ability to create innovative solutions. As technology continues to advance, the demand for expertise in actuator integration will only grow, making this knowledge an invaluable asset in the field of electronics and automation.

Integrating Sensors and Actuators in Projects

Integrating sensors and actuators in electronic projects is a fundamental aspect of creating responsive and interactive systems. Sensors are devices that detect changes in the environment and convert those changes into signals that can be processed. Actuators, on the other hand, are components that execute actions based on signals received from control systems. Together, they form a crucial interface between the physical world and electronic devices, enabling a wide range of applications from simple home automation systems to complex robotics.

The first step in integrating sensors and actuators is understanding the types of sensors available. Common categories include temperature sensors, humidity sensors, motion detectors, and light sensors, among others. Each type of sensor operates on specific principles and is suited for particular applications. For instance, temperature sensors like thermistors or thermocouples provide critical data for climate control systems, while motion sensors can trigger alarms or automate lighting in smart homes. Knowing the appropriate sensor for your project is essential for achieving desired functionality.

Once the right sensors are selected, the next phase involves connecting them to a microcontroller or a microprocessor. This is where the integration takes shape. A microcontroller acts as the brain of the system, processing the information received from the sensors and executing commands to the actuators. Typical platforms for these integrations include Arduino, Raspberry Pi, and ESP8266. These platforms provide libraries and support for a variety of sensors and actuators, allowing for streamlined coding and rapid prototyping. Learning how to interface these components is a vital skill for any tech enthusiast or builder.

After establishing sensor connections, programming the microcontroller is essential to define how it interprets sensor data and controls actuators. This programming can involve writing code that processes input signals, implements decision-making algorithms, and sends output commands to actuators. For example, a temperature sensor might be programmed to activate a fan when a certain temperature threshold is exceeded. Familiarity with programming languages such as C, Python, or JavaScript, depending on the platform, will significantly enhance the project's functionality and responsiveness.

Finally, testing and iterating the integrated system is crucial for ensuring reliability and performance. This phase includes observing how the sensors respond to environmental changes and how effectively the actuators perform their designated tasks. Debugging any issues that arise during testing is necessary to fine-tune the system. Furthermore, seeking feedback and conducting iterative improvements will enhance the project's overall effectiveness. By mastering the integration of sensors and actuators, students and emerging tech leaders can create innovative solutions that bridge the gap between digital and physical realms, paving the way for a smarter future.

CHAPTER 9

POWER SUPPLY AND MANAGEMENT

Types of Power Supplies

Power supplies are crucial components in electronic circuits, responsible for providing the necessary voltage and current for the operation of devices. They can be categorized into various types based on their design, functionality, and application. Understanding these types is essential for computer students, engineers, and tech founders as they navigate the landscape of electronics and design effective systems for their projects.

The first major category of power supplies is linear power supplies. These devices operate by using a transformer to step down the voltage to a desired level. They typically include a rectifier, filter, and regulator to provide a stable output voltage. Linear power supplies are known for their simplicity and reliability, making them ideal for applications where low noise is critical. However, they are less efficient than other types, especially when high voltage conversion is required, as they dissipate excess voltage as heat.

Switching power supplies represent another significant type. Unlike linear supplies, switching power supplies use high-frequency switching techniques to convert input voltage to a desired output voltage. This method allows for greater efficiency and smaller size, as less heat is generated during the conversion process. They are widely used in computer systems and other electronic devices where space and power efficiency are essential. However, the design of switching power supplies can be more complex, and they may introduce electromagnetic interference that must be managed.

Uninterruptible power supplies (UPS) are specialized devices designed to provide backup power during outages. They typically combine a battery with a power supply to ensure that electronic devices continue to operate even when the main power source fails. UPS systems are critical for protecting sensitive equipment, such as servers and medical devices, from data loss and damage caused by power interruptions. Understanding the operation of UPS systems is vital for tech founders and engineers who need to ensure reliability in their products.

Finally, there are renewable energy power supplies, which harness natural resources such as solar, wind, or hydroelectric power to generate electricity. These systems often include inverters and battery storage to provide a stable and continuous power output. With the growing emphasis on sustainability and reducing carbon footprints, renewable energy power supplies are becoming increasingly important in modern electronics. Knowledge of these systems is essential for future tech leaders who are focusing on innovative and environmentally friendly solutions in their designs.

Battery Technologies

Battery technologies are a cornerstone of modern electronics, playing a critical role in the functionality and portability of devices. At the heart of this technology lies the fundamental principle of electrochemistry, where chemical energy is converted into electrical energy. The most common types of batteries include lead-acid, nickel-cadmium (NiCd), nickel-metal hydride (NiMH), and lithium-ion (Li-ion). Each of these technologies has its unique characteristics, advantages, and limitations, making them suitable for different applications ranging from portable electronics to electric vehicles.

Lead-acid batteries, one of the oldest and most established types, are often used in automotive applications due to their robustness and low cost. These batteries consist of lead dioxide and sponge lead plates submerged in sulfuric acid. While they offer high surge currents, they are heavy and have a lower energy density compared to newer technologies. Their lifespan can be limited by factors such as cycling and temperature, but they remain a reliable option for applications requiring high power over short periods.

Nickel-cadmium batteries provided a significant advancement over lead-acid systems, offering better energy density and rechargeability. However, they are increasingly being phased out due to environmental concerns related to cadmium, a toxic heavy metal. NiCd batteries are known for their ability to perform well in extreme temperatures and their long cycle life. Despite their drawbacks, such as memory effect and self-discharge rates, they were widely used in portable tools and electronic devices until more advanced alternatives emerged.

Nickel-metal hydride batteries emerged as an improved option, offering greater capacity and reduced environmental impact compared to their nickel-cadmium counterparts. NiMH batteries are commonly used in hybrid vehicles and consumer electronics, providing a good balance between cost, performance, and capacity. They have largely supplanted NiCd batteries in many applications, although they still suffer from self-discharge issues. Their ability to deliver consistent power makes them a popular choice in various devices, including digital cameras and power tools.

Lithium-ion batteries have revolutionized the industry with their high energy density, low weight, and long cycle life. These batteries are now the standard in mobile devices, laptops, and electric vehicles. Lithium-ion technology uses a lithium salt as the electrolyte and can be designed in various configurations, such as cylindrical or prismatic cells. With advancements in materials and battery management systems, Li-ion batteries have become more efficient and safer, leading to innovations in energy storage solutions. As research continues to evolve, future battery technologies, including solid-state and lithium-sulfur batteries, promise even greater performance and sustainability, paving the way for the next generation of electronic devices and applications.

Power Management Techniques

Power management techniques are critical in the design and operation of electronic systems, especially as devices become increasingly portable and energy-efficient. These techniques aim to optimize the use of energy, extending battery life in portable devices and minimizing energy consumption in larger systems. Understanding the various strategies employed in power management can significantly enhance the performance and sustainability of electronic devices.

One of the fundamental techniques is dynamic voltage and frequency scaling (DVFS), which adjusts the voltage and frequency of a processor based on the current workload. By lowering these parameters during periods of low activity, DVFS can reduce power consumption without sacrificing performance. This technique is widely used in modern computing systems, particularly in mobile devices, where battery life is paramount. Implementing DVFS requires careful monitoring of workload demands and can involve complex algorithms that predict the optimal voltage and frequency settings.

Another important power management technique is sleep mode implementation. Many electronic devices are designed to enter a low-power state when not in use, significantly reducing energy consumption. There are various sleep modes, such as standby and hibernate, each with different power-saving attributes. Designers must consider the trade-offs between power savings and the time taken to resume full functionality. Effective sleep mode strategies are essential for devices like laptops and smartphones, where user convenience and energy efficiency must be balanced.

Power gating is another advanced technique used to control

power delivery to different components selectively. By turning off power to inactive sections of a circuit while keeping other parts operational, power gating can lead to substantial energy savings. This technique is particularly useful in integrated circuits, where multiple functional blocks can be independently powered. The challenge lies in implementing power gating without disrupting the overall functionality of the device, necessitating robust design methodologies and testing.

Lastly, energy harvesting is gaining traction as a complementary power management strategy. This technique involves capturing energy from the environment, such as solar, thermal, or kinetic energy, and converting it into electrical power. Incorporating energy harvesting solutions can significantly enhance the sustainability of electronic devices, particularly in applications where traditional power sources are impractical. However, integrating these systems requires a solid understanding of both power management and energy conversion technologies, making it a vital area of study for future tech leaders.

CHAPTER 10

PRACTICAL PROJECTS AND APPLICATIONS

Building Simple Circuits

Building simple circuits is foundational for anyone venturing into the world of electronics. Understanding the basic principles behind circuit design helps to establish a solid grounding in both theory and practice. A simple circuit typically consists of a power source, a load, and connecting wires. Common components used in these circuits include resistors, capacitors, diodes, and transistors. By learning to build simple circuits, students and budding tech leaders can develop practical skills that will be essential in more complex projects.

To begin constructing a simple circuit, one must first select a power source. This can be a battery, a solar panel, or a plug-in power supply. The power source provides the necessary voltage and current for the circuit to operate. Next, understanding the role of the load is crucial. The load is the component that consumes electrical energy, such as a light bulb or a motor. The interaction between the power source and the load is where the fundamental principles of voltage, current, and resistance come into play, as described by Ohm's Law.

Once the power source and load are established, the next step is to incorporate additional components to tailor the circuit's functionality. Resistors can be added to control the current flowing through the circuit. Capacitors can store and release energy, which is particularly useful in timing applications or filtering signals. Diodes allow current to flow in one direction, protecting sensitive components from potential damage. Transistors can act as switches or amplifiers, enabling more complex functionalities within the circuit.

The physical construction of the circuit can be done using a breadboard or a PCB (printed circuit board). A breadboard is an excellent tool for beginners, as it allows for easy modification and experimentation without the need for soldering. Students can practice connecting components, ensuring they understand the flow of electricity and how to create effective connections. As confidence grows, transitioning to PCB design introduces an essential aspect of professional electronics development, allowing for more permanent and compact circuit solutions.

Documenting the process of building simple circuits is equally important. Keeping a log of circuit designs, component values, and results helps in troubleshooting and refining future projects. Sharing these logs with peers fosters collaboration and enhances collective learning. By mastering the art of building simple circuits, computer students and tech founders gain invaluable experience that serves as a stepping stone to more advanced electronic projects, ultimately equipping them to innovate and lead in the rapidly evolving tech landscape.

Intermediate Projects for Skill Development

Intermediate projects in electronics serve as a bridge between foundational knowledge and advanced applications, providing students and budding tech leaders with hands-on experience that enhances their understanding of key concepts. Engaging in these projects not only solidifies theoretical knowledge but also fosters problem-solving skills, creativity, and critical thinking. The following intermediate projects are designed to challenge students while reinforcing essential skills necessary for a successful career in technology and engineering.

One notable project is the design and construction of a digital thermometer. This project involves using thermistors or temperature sensors, such as the LM35, interfaced with a microcontroller like the Arduino. Students will learn about analog-to-digital conversion, data representation, and interfacing sensors with microcontrollers. By incorporating an LCD display, they will also gain valuable experience in working with visual output devices. This project not only allows for hands-on experience with coding and circuit design but also promotes an understanding of environmental monitoring and data analysis.

Another engaging project is the creation of a simple home automation system. Utilizing components like relays, sensors, and a microcontroller, students can design a system that controls lights, fans, or other appliances based on environmental inputs or user commands. This project introduces the concepts of IoT (Internet of Things) and wireless communication, as students can implement remote control features using Bluetooth or Wi-Fi. By working on this project, students will enhance their skills in programming, circuit integration, and user interface design, which are crucial in today's technology landscape.

Building a basic robotic arm is another excellent intermediate project that combines mechanics with electronics. Students will learn to control servos using a microcontroller, allowing them to manipulate the arm's movements. This project emphasizes principles of robotics, such as kinematics and control systems, while also providing insight into the integration of hardware and software. Students can further enhance this project by incorporating sensors for object detection or implementing a graphical user interface to control the arm remotely, thus expanding their programming and engineering skills.

Lastly, constructing a sound-activated LED display can be an exciting and educational project. By utilizing microphones to detect sound levels and microcontrollers to control LED patterns, students can explore sound processing and visual representation. This project challenges students to think creatively about how to interact with their environment and present information in engaging ways. It also hones their skills in circuit design, programming, and debugging, essential abilities for any tech-focused career.

These intermediate projects not only serve as excellent learning experiences but also prepare students for future challenges in their careers. By working on practical applications, students can develop a deeper understanding of electronics, improve their technical skills, and cultivate a mindset geared towards innovation and problem-solving. Engaging in these projects can ignite a passion for technology, inspire creativity, and lay a strong foundation for future endeavors in the ever-evolving field of electronics.

Capstone Projects for Tech Leaders

Capstone projects serve as a critical component in the development of future tech leaders, particularly in the field of electronics. These projects allow students to apply theoretical knowledge in practical settings, bridging the gap between classroom learning and real-world application. For computer students and aspiring engineers, capstone projects offer a unique opportunity to explore innovations in basic electronics while honing essential skills such as problem-solving, teamwork, and project management. Engaging in these projects not only enhances technical expertise but also fosters creativity and critical thinking, which are crucial for leadership roles in technology.

A well-defined capstone project should start with identifying a relevant problem or challenge in the electronics field. Students can explore a variety of themes, such as energy efficiency, automation, or smart technologies. For instance, creating a prototype for an energy-efficient device could address the growing concern of environmental sustainability while providing hands-on experience with circuit design and component selection. By focusing on real-world issues, students can develop solutions that not only demonstrate their technical abilities but also contribute positively to society, thereby enhancing their appeal as future tech leaders.

Collaboration is another vital aspect of capstone projects. Many successful projects are the result of teamwork, where diverse skills and perspectives combine to innovate effectively. Students can form interdisciplinary groups, bringing together individuals with varying expertise in software, hardware, and design. This collaborative approach not only enriches the learning experience but also mirrors workplace dynamics in the tech industry, where cross-functional teams are essential for successful project execution. Through teamwork, students can learn valuable lessons in communication and cooperation, which are indispensable qualities for tech leaders.

Documentation and presentation of the capstone project are equally important. Students must systematically record their research, design processes, and outcomes to create a comprehensive report. This documentation serves as a reflection of their efforts and can be a critical asset when showcasing their work to potential employers or investors. Additionally, presenting the project to peers, faculty, and industry professionals helps develop public speaking skills and the ability to articulate complex ideas clearly. This experience prepares students for future opportunities where they may need to advocate for their projects or innovations in a professional setting.

Lastly, capstone projects can serve as a launching pad for future endeavors in the tech industry. The skills and knowledge gained through these projects can lead to internships, job offers, or even the foundation of a startup. By demonstrating their ability to conceive and execute a project from start to finish, students can position themselves as capable candidates in a competitive job market. Moreover, these projects can spark ideas for further research or development, encouraging students to continue exploring the field of electronics beyond their academic studies. As such, capstone projects not only culminate academic journeys but also lay the groundwork for successful careers as tech leaders.

CHAPTER 11

FUTURE TRENDS IN ELECTRONICS

Emerging Technologies in Electronics

Emerging technologies in electronics are driving innovations that reshape industries and enhance everyday life. One of the most significant advancements is the development of flexible electronics. This technology allows for the creation of lightweight, bendable circuits that can be integrated into various substrates, including textiles and packaging materials. Flexible electronics open up new possibilities for wearable devices, smart clothing, and healthcare applications, enabling continuous monitoring of vital signs without compromising comfort. The ability to produce electronics that conform to different shapes and surfaces has the potential to revolutionize how we interact with technology in our daily lives.

Another noteworthy trend is the rise of quantum computing. Unlike classical computers that process information using bits, quantum computers leverage the principles of quantum mechanics to perform calculations at unprecedented speeds. This technology can solve complex problems that are currently beyond the reach of traditional computing systems, particularly in fields such as cryptography, drug discovery, and optimization problems. As quantum hardware and algorithms continue to evolve, they are expected to significantly impact various sectors, offering solutions that were once considered impossible.

Additionally, the integration of artificial intelligence (AI) in electronic systems is transforming the way devices operate. AI algorithms can optimize the performance of electronic components, improving energy efficiency and functionality. Machine learning techniques enable devices to learn from user behavior, providing personalized experiences and automation.

This synergy between AI and electronics is evident in smart home devices, autonomous vehicles, and industrial automation, showcasing the potential for increased efficiency and enhanced user interaction.

The advancement of Internet of Things (IoT) technology is another critical area in electronics. IoT connects everyday devices to the internet, allowing for seamless communication and data exchange. This connectivity enables remote monitoring, control, and automation of various systems, from home appliances to industrial machinery. As IoT continues to expand, challenges such as security and data privacy must be addressed to ensure safe and reliable operation. The integration of IoT in various industries promises to enhance operational efficiency and create new business models.

Lastly, advancements in energy storage technologies, particularly in batteries, are essential for the future of electronics. The demand for renewable energy sources and electric vehicles has accelerated the need for efficient energy storage solutions. Innovations in solid-state batteries and lithium-sulfur technologies are paving the way for higher energy densities, faster charging times, and improved safety. As these technologies mature, they will play a crucial role in enabling the widespread adoption of energy-efficient devices and sustainable energy systems, further driving the evolution of electronics in the coming years.

The Role of Electronics in Future Innovations

The role of electronics in future innovations is increasingly pivotal, as advancements in this field serve as the backbone of modern technology. Electronics are not merely components of devices; they are the essential building blocks that enable the functionality, efficiency, and performance of a wide range of applications. From the microchips that power smartphones to the sensors that drive autonomous vehicles, the impact of electronics permeates every layer of contemporary tech infrastructure. As computer students, engineers, and tech founders look ahead, understanding the trajectory of electronic innovations will be crucial for driving future developments.

One of the most significant areas where electronics are set to play a transformative role is in the Internet of Things (IoT). The proliferation of smart devices and interconnected systems relies heavily on advanced electronic components, including sensors, microcontrollers, and communication interfaces. These elements facilitate the collection and exchange of data, enabling more intelligent systems capable of analyzing and responding to real-time information. As IoT continues to evolve, the demand for more sophisticated electronic solutions will grow, driving innovation in areas such as low-power design, miniaturization, and enhanced connectivity protocols.

Moreover, electronics are at the forefront of the development of artificial intelligence (AI) and machine learning technologies. The computational power required for AI applications is largely derived from advanced electronics, particularly in the form of GPUs and specialized processors designed for deep learning tasks. As AI becomes integrated into various sectors—including healthcare, finance, and manufacturing—the need for efficient electronic systems that can handle complex algorithms and large datasets will be paramount. This intersection of electronics and AI presents unique opportunities for future engineers and tech entrepreneurs to create groundbreaking solutions that can reshape industries.

Sustainability is another critical area where electronics will play a vital role in future innovations. As global concerns about climate change and resource depletion mount, the electronics industry is increasingly focusing on developing energy-efficient technologies and sustainable manufacturing practices. Innovations such as flexible electronics, energy-harvesting devices, and recyclable materials are emerging to address these challenges. For tech leaders, understanding how to implement these sustainable practices in electronic design and production will not only contribute to environmental goals but also meet the growing consumer demand for eco-friendly products.

Finally, the ongoing advancements in semiconductor technology will continue to revolutionize various sectors. The development of new materials, such as graphene and silicon carbide, promises to enhance the performance and efficiency of electronic devices significantly. As the limits of traditional silicon-based components are reached, exploring these alternative materials will pave the way for the next generation of electronics, enabling faster processing speeds, reduced power consumption, and improved thermal management. For computer students and engineers, staying informed about these trends is essential for leveraging new technologies and driving future innovations in the field.

Preparing for a Career in Electronics

Preparing for a career in electronics requires a solid foundation in both theoretical knowledge and practical skills. As technology continues to evolve, professionals in the electronics field must adapt to new developments and innovations. Understanding the principles of electronics, including circuit design, signal processing, and system integration, is essential. Students should focus on building a strong grasp of fundamental concepts through coursework, self-study, and hands-on projects. Engaging with textbooks, online courses, and tutorials can provide valuable insights into the core topics of electronics, fostering a deeper understanding of how various components interact within a system.

In addition to academic knowledge, practical experience plays a crucial role in preparing for a career in electronics. Students should seek opportunities to work on projects that involve circuit design, prototyping, and troubleshooting. Joining clubs or organizations focused on electronics can enhance skills through collaborative projects and competitions. Internships or co-op programs with electronics companies can also provide real-world experience, allowing students to apply their knowledge in professional settings. This hands-on experience is invaluable, as it equips future tech leaders with problem-solving skills and an understanding of industry practices.

Networking is another important aspect of preparing for a career in electronics. Building connections with professionals in the field can lead to mentorship opportunities, job prospects, and collaborations on projects. Attending industry conferences, workshops, and seminars can help students meet experts and peers who share their interests. Online platforms and social media groups focused on electronics can also serve as resources for networking and staying updated on industry trends. Engaging with the community can provide insights into the skills and qualifications that employers value, informing students' career decisions.

Staying current with technological advancements is vital in the fast-paced world of electronics. Students should cultivate a habit of continuous learning by exploring emerging technologies such as the Internet of Things (IoT), artificial intelligence, and renewable energy systems. Subscribing to relevant journals, following industry news, and participating in online forums can help students stay informed about the latest developments. This proactive approach to learning not only enhances technical knowledge but also demonstrates a commitment to professional growth, an attribute that employers highly regard.

Lastly, developing soft skills is equally important in the electronics field. Communication, teamwork, and project management are essential for successful collaboration in technical environments. Students should seek opportunities to enhance these skills through group projects, presentations, and leadership roles within organizations. Employers often look for candidates who not only possess technical expertise but also demonstrate the ability to work effectively within diverse teams. By focusing on both technical skills and interpersonal abilities, future tech leaders can position themselves as well-rounded professionals ready to tackle the challenges of the electronics industry.

CHAPTER 12

CONCLUSION

Recap of Key Concepts

In the journey through the fundamentals of electronics, several key concepts serve as the foundation for understanding how electronic systems operate. This recap emphasizes the essential principles that every computer student, engineer, or tech founder should grasp. The interplay between voltage, current, and resistance, defined by Ohm's Law, is a primary concept. It illustrates how these three components are interrelated, allowing for the analysis and design of electrical circuits. Understanding this relationship is crucial for troubleshooting and optimizing circuit performance, which is a core skill in electronics.

Another significant concept is the distinction between analog and digital signals. Analog signals are continuous and can take any value within a given range, while digital signals are discrete and represented by binary values. This distinction is vital for students and professionals working with various technologies, including sensors, microcontrollers, and communication systems. Grasping how these signals function and interact with electronic components is essential for designing efficient and effective systems, whether in consumer electronics or industrial applications.

The role of components such as resistors, capacitors, and inductors cannot be overlooked. Each component has unique characteristics and functions within a circuit. Resistors limit current flow, capacitors store and release energy, and inductors create magnetic fields in response to electrical current. Understanding how to select and combine these components is fundamental for creating circuits that meet specific requirements. This knowledge allows future tech leaders to innovate and develop new technologies that can solve real-world challenges.

In addition to components, the concept of circuit design and analysis is a critical area of focus. Techniques such as series and parallel configurations, as well as the use of circuit simulation tools, provide students with the skills needed to visualize and test circuit behavior before physical implementation. Mastery of these techniques not only enhances problem-solving abilities but also fosters creativity in developing new electronic solutions. As technology evolves, these design principles remain relevant and adaptable to emerging trends.

Lastly, the importance of safety and best practices in electronics cannot be overstated. Understanding the risks associated with working with electrical components and systems is essential for preventing accidents and injuries. Proper grounding, circuit protection, and safe handling procedures are fundamental concepts that should be ingrained in every aspiring tech leader's training. By prioritizing safety, students and professionals can ensure that their innovations contribute positively to technological advancement while safeguarding themselves and others in the field.

The Importance of Continuous Learning

Continuous learning is essential for anyone involved in the field of electronics, especially for computer students, engineers, and tech founders. The rapid evolution of technology means that knowledge can quickly become outdated. New theories, methodologies, and tools are constantly being developed, requiring professionals to stay informed and adaptable. Embracing a mindset of lifelong learning enables individuals to remain competitive in a fast-paced industry, ensuring they can leverage the latest advancements to enhance their work and drive innovation.

The importance of continuous learning is underscored by the diverse applications of electronics in modern society. From consumer electronics to complex industrial systems, the integration of electronic components is ubiquitous. As new challenges emerge, such as increasing energy efficiency, improving connectivity, and advancing automation, it is crucial for individuals in the field to acquire new skills and knowledge to address these issues effectively. Staying abreast of industry trends and emerging technologies allows tech leaders to make informed decisions and implement solutions that can significantly impact their organizations and the broader community.

Moreover, continuous learning fosters creativity and problem-solving abilities. Engaging with new concepts and technologies inspires innovative thinking and encourages individuals to explore unconventional solutions to complex problems. For instance, understanding the principles of machine learning can open new avenues for electronics design, while familiarity with sustainable practices can lead to the development of greener technologies. When students and professionals commit to learning, they not only enhance their own capabilities but also contribute to the collective knowledge of their teams and organizations.

Networking with peers and industry experts is another critical aspect of continuous learning. Attending conferences, workshops, and seminars provides opportunities to exchange ideas, gain insights from thought leaders, and collaborate on projects. These interactions can lead to mentorship opportunities and partnerships that may not have been possible otherwise. Additionally, participating in online forums and discussion groups allows individuals to share their experiences and learn from the challenges faced by others in the field, creating a vibrant community of practice that benefits all members.

Finally, fostering a culture of continuous learning within organizations can lead to overall success and sustainability.

Companies that invest in the ongoing education of their employees not only benefit from enhanced skills and knowledge but also cultivate a motivated and engaged workforce. Encouraging team members to pursue learning opportunities, whether through formal education or self-directed study, can lead to higher job satisfaction and retention rates. In an industry characterized by rapid change, organizations that prioritize continuous learning are better positioned to adapt and thrive in the face of new challenges and opportunities.

Resources for Further Study

In pursuing a deeper understanding of basic electronics, students and tech enthusiasts have access to a wealth of resources that can significantly enhance their learning experience. Textbooks remain a cornerstone for foundational knowledge, and several titles are particularly well-suited for beginners. "The Art of Electronics" by Paul Horowitz and Winfield Hill provides a comprehensive introduction while offering practical insights through real-world applications. Additionally, "Make: Electronics" by Charles Platt promotes hands-on experimentation, making it an excellent choice for those who prefer learning by doing. These texts not only cover theoretical principles but also guide readers through practical projects that reinforce concepts.

Online platforms have emerged as invaluable resources for modern learners. Websites like Khan Academy and Coursera offer courses in basic electronics that cater to different learning styles. These platforms provide video tutorials, quizzes, and interactive components that help students grasp complex ideas more effectively. Furthermore, YouTube channels such as EEVblog and GreatScott! deliver engaging content ranging from product reviews to circuit design tutorials. These resources allow learners to visualize concepts and see real-world applications, which can be crucial for retaining knowledge.

For those who prefer a more structured learning environment, community colleges and technical schools often offer workshops and certification programs in electronics. These courses typically combine classroom instruction with hands-on lab work, facilitating skill acquisition in a collaborative setting. Networking with peers and instructors in these environments not only enhances learning but also fosters connections that can be beneficial for future career opportunities. Students are encouraged to explore local institutions that provide these resources to enrich their educational journey.

In addition to formal education and online resources, professional organizations play a significant role in the development of aspiring electronics professionals. Groups such as the Institute of Electrical and Electronics Engineers (IEEE) offer access to journals, conferences, and networking opportunities. Membership can provide students with insights into industry trends, access to research papers, and platforms to connect with experienced professionals. Engaging with these organizations can help students stay informed about advancements in technology and best practices in the field.

Finally, practical experience remains one of the most effective ways to solidify knowledge in electronics. Students are encouraged to participate in maker spaces or local electronics clubs where they can collaborate on projects and share ideas. Engaging in competitions, such as robotics contests, can also provide valuable hands-on experience while fostering teamwork and problem-solving skills. By leveraging these diverse resources, future tech leaders can build a strong foundation in basic electronics, equipping themselves with the knowledge and skills necessary to thrive in the ever-evolving technological landscape.

ACKNOWLEDGEMENT

No journey of leadership is undertaken alone, and the completion of *The CEO Mindset: Building Resilience in Tech* is a testament to the incredible support, guidance, and inspiration I have received from many individuals along the way.

First and foremost, I am deeply grateful to my family, whose unwavering belief in me has been a source of strength and motivation. Your patience, encouragement, and love have been my foundation through the highs and lows of my entrepreneurial journey.

To my co-founders, team members, and colleagues at gcodecloud GmbH and Mega Phonebook Nig—this book is as much yours as it is mine. Your dedication, creativity, and resilience have shaped our success, and I am privileged to lead alongside such talented and passionate individuals. Thank you for believing in our vision and for your tireless efforts to bring it to life.

I would like to extend my heartfelt gratitude to the mentors, advisors, and industry leaders who have guided me throughout my career. Your wisdom and insights have been invaluable, and your willingness to share your experiences has helped me grow not only as a leader but also as a person.

A special thanks to the investors, clients, and partners who have placed their trust in our mission and supported our endeavors. Your confidence in our work has been a driving force behind our growth and success.

To my friends and peers in the tech and entrepreneurial community, thank you for your camaraderie, support, and collaboration. Your shared experiences and stories have enriched my understanding of leadership and resilience in the tech industry.

Finally, I am grateful to every reader who picks up this book. Your pursuit of growth, leadership, and innovation is a testament to the spirit of resilience that drives the tech industry forward. I hope this book serves as a guide, a source of inspiration, and a reminder that with the right mindset, every challenge is an opportunity for growth.

Thank you all for being part of this journey. Your impact on my life and career is immeasurable, and I am forever grateful.

— Golf Ofuka

ABOUT THE AUTHOR

Golf Ofuka

Golf Ofuka is the dynamic CEO and Founder of gcodecloud GmbH and Mega Phonebook Nig, recognized for his innovative approach to technology and business. His career and entrepreneurial journey highlight his expertise in the software and IT industry, alongside a robust knowledge of business strategy, development, and market positioning. Based in Berlin, Germany, Golf leverages his strong technical foundation and a sharp business acumen to spearhead ventures that bridge technological innovation with market needs.

Background and Leadership
Golf's career path reflects a blend of technology mastery and entrepreneurial insight, making him a valuable leader in today's fast-paced digital landscape. As the CEO and driving force behind gcodecloud GmbH, he leads a team that is transforming software solutions for modern enterprises. His leadership is marked by a deep commitment to fostering innovation within his organization and a clear vision for scaling products and services that meet the evolving demands of global markets.

www.ingramcontent.com/pod-product-compliance
Lightning Source LLC
Chambersburg PA
CBHW070346230526
45471CB00006B/2443